MIRRORE

Emerging Poets Anthology

STAR INVESTMENT STRATEGIES LLC

DEDICATION

This book is dedicated to the unheard creative minds of the time and master poets of the past that paved the way. Though poetry is a hard genre to survive in, it is the most descriptive, expressive, and heart-felt genre ever put on paper. These are the mindless ramblings of creative dreamers. With words, all dreams come to life.

"Letters are meaningless unless put together correctly. Words are worthless unless backed by truth. Sentences are handed out and judged accordingly, but only genuinely honest men or women can create writings that change the world forever." –Paul Morabito

CONTENTS

ACKNOWLEDGMENTS

I would like to thank all the outstanding poets for contributing to the first volume of the Mirrored Voices Anthology. This collection has a nice array of topics and styles that hit across all the major emotions. I am honored to have published this book with such a fine group of creative minds from across the globe.

Paul Morabito

Paul Morabito is an American born fiction/nonfiction author that was raised in a close knit Italian-American family in the state of New Jersey where pasta and meatball Sundays were always commonplace. He had an amazing childhood until the sudden tragic death of his dear brother, Carmelo. It was this event that stirred the will and desire to succeed physically, mentally and artistically to make his brother and family proud. Paul took on and enjoyed martial arts where he excelled at a very young age. Determined to find another passion, Paul stumbled upon chess and another hidden musical talent which made him form a local band with childhood friends. He soon mastered and played lead guitar which became an extension of himself for many years to come as an accomplished musician. His love for music grew and still remains to this day as does his desire to release a solo album in the future.

On the path to achieving a degree in pharmacy, Paul discovered a great interest in English Literature where he focused on masterpiece tragedies and works such as those written by Shakespeare, Chaucer, and Poe. Little was known that this would spark a fire of inspiration to jump into the world of writing where creative minds blossom and run free.

His career took over a decade long hiatus but was blessed with two beautiful princesses who are his everything. The urge to continue with his dream led to the release of two latest projects in the same year, both stemming from an Evangelical Christian background. The author's faith in God remains strong and he entrusts his life, children and career in His hands. Paul plans to continue writing across all fictional genres and start filming his first cinematic production.

Works to date include Making Money In Today's Economy, Plane Hell: The Hell's Plane Amulet, Plane Hell: The Amulet of the dead, The Preying Grounds, An Angel from Above, Fallen Beloved and Poetic Delusions Book 1 and 2.

http://www.Paul-Morabito.com

1 LOVE FREEZE

I have not known love until I met you.
This knight's armor pierced straight through.
Your voice alone can sooth this ferocious lion's rage.
Free this unhappy life sentence cage.
Your whisper is the spring breeze in ear.
The laugh in my hopeless cheer.
Your warm touch is the burning heat of sun.
First steps in journeys just begun.

I have not known calmness until I met you.
This nervous shipwreck floats anew.
Your song brings tranquility to treacherous seas.
Shows this wretched old bird the bees.
Your heart pumps love through my veins.
Cleanses my soul, removes life's stains.
Your kiss is cure to all disease.
Even time your love does freeze.

Paul Morabito ©

2 THAT JOYFUL SUMMER

Summer has gone and past.
Another season cast by the way side.
The warmth of loving sun will soon dwindle.
Like the memories of our fun time spent together.
Laying on the beach.
Gazing out into the wavy ocean blue.
Making castles of sand that slowly dissipate with each passing
wind.
Listening to the roaring crashes of nature that hold mankind
in contempt.
And all along the welcome distractions make me think only of
you.
Holding your soft hands in mine as we roam the seashore.
Occasionally stopping to admire the beauty of one another's
presence.
As the excitement of wondrous colored shells are discovered
at our moist feet.
Children's laughter brings us back to our youthful years.
When we were carefree, innocent, and ignorant of the hateful
world.
That precious summer was the reason for living.
The purpose for awaking and breathing the fresh air of love.
Though the joys, laughs, smiles, caresses and daily
experiences will soon part as history.
They will remain close to heart and published eternally.

Paul Morabito ©

3 WALL OF CHAMPIONS

I'm blinded by the gold array of victory.
Monuments of achievement.
Testament to worthiness.
The true artifacts of a born winner.

I am in awe and dwell in their shadows.
The hard work and discipline alone cuts many from
ownership.
The rightful prizes of excellence.
A true collection of human dominance.

Just a rare few can achieve such greatness.
To fill a room with astonishing feats of untold stories.
Do not be fooled by the silence.
Each statue of perfection has its own tale to tell.

Four of hated rivalry.
Three of friendly competition.
Two of oh so close heartbreak.
And the one of joyous pain that ended my career.

Games won before such rowdy crowds.
Now collect dust and are soon forgotten.
Some are haplessly thrown away.
Broken.

For every trophy destroyed.
There is a champion removed from the annals of history.
For every one admired.
There is an athlete's life marveled.

Splayed across the walls like tombstones.
They hover above.
Wishing only to be loved and remembered.
After all these years of trying to choose my favorite.
I finally realized.
My most desired of all.
Was the one I didn't bring home.

Paul Morabito ©

4 THE WINDOW

From the outside looking in.
Tales of love lost soon begin.
Through holidays and joyous seasons.
I'm not there for all false reasons.
Trust lost and oath betrayed.
Soon new love will be dismayed.

As the kids laugh and play.
I'm all alone and here I stay.
Standing frostbit in the cold.
Should've listened to what parents told.

Not to trust a hardened maid.
That just lies, cheats and stealing craves.
Holding all to blind eye's ignorance.
While inside ruled by selfish dominance.

New life built on false hope.
Kid's lives shattered while daddy's played the dope.
Now imposter takes my place.
Tricked dearly by wicked false face.
Don't feel bad for I, but for other.

To whom lies were told of honest bride and righteous mother.
For evenings of sinful bliss.

Family wrecked and innocent lives dismissed.

Now I stand outside stained and broken window.
Rather freeze here than be warm where sin grows.
Secrets kept hidden from friends in deep blizzard snows.
Wait till warm Spring comes because Heaven knows.

Paul Morabito ©

5 DYING INSIDE

Cries fall upon deaf ears.
No one can feel the hurt.
No one can see the pain.
Hidden behind this mask of strength.
I am portrayed as a rock.
But mountains and stone crumble.
Mighty walls tumble.
The torture at times is too much.
The heart pounds but is dying.
Eyes dry but crying.
Blank stares and not present.
Heavy mind and heart like cement.
Drowning to the deepest oceans.
Where the daylight sun can't penetrate.
My aura reeks of filth.
Withering the plant beside me.
Bending it into gloominess.
My mask casts a shadow upon it.
Dooming the fruits of life.
I'm sorry but this isn't really me.
It's a mirage.
I'm half I used to be.
Should be ashamed to wear this cover.
Afraid to speak with family or lover.

So yet it dies.
Soaking in my misery.
Fight young one.
Fight.
Deeply dig down those outstretched roots.
Don't succumb to my misfortune.
Don't be the sharp edged leaf that death splits this rock in two.
Be the bright petal of hope that shines through and through.
I now remove this mask for you to live.
Honor.
Love.
Truth.
Unselfishness.
There is nothing else.
This poor crumbling rock can give.

Paul Morabito ©

6 WALK WITH ME

Taken all away.
Not owning anything but these wretched striped clothes.
Live another day.
For what?
Innocently convicted under false pretenses.
There isn't anything else worth saying.
No use explaining.
All things stripped from me.
I leave how I was born.
This time, noose worn.
Guess my name drew first.
While breathing life eternally cursed.
Striving just to fall.
Tried and gave it all.
To some, life gives.
But all it did was take.
Suicide is sin.
Heaven gates future won't bring.
Just sit here in the dark.
Awaiting light from Heaven's spark.
Minutes pass.
Hours.
Days.
Weeks.
Years.

No use fighting tears.
All spent.
Just like money.
Love.
Joy.
Cigarettes.
Everything good.
The darkness consumes.
The void too big to fill.
Rather this than poison pill.
I stare at pictures on prison wall.
Remembering days when times were happy.
So far away.
So. So. Far.
As though they never happened.
All these decades with nothing to show.
Take my hand officer.
It's time to go.
One last time to hear the wolves' laughter.
While strolling down death row's slaughter.

Paul Morabito ©

7 NUMBERED DAYS

From birth to death.
The grains of sand are counted.
Do what we may.
Say what we wish.
The outcome is certain.
It is the in between we can alter.
It is this precious timeline which determines who is
remembered or forgotten.
Honored or called rotten.
The bonds we formed in life will be what was valued most.
For all the gold in the world will be worthless upon gasping
last breaths.
It is through this journey of temptation that we are judged.
The most minute of timelines in ages past.
To get a chance at eternal life.
The Holy Grail.
The key to infinity that exists by confessing words of faith.
That repels and rebukes evil.
Oh yes.
The days are numbered.
If spent loving, working or foolishly slumbered.
Live for now with righteousness and honor.
Touch lives and bless one another.
Don't let the reaper a second steal.
While reading the clock is ticking.
Words of wisdom might help your thinking.

To spur a bucket list action.
To clear your mind of a worldly distraction.
The purpose in life each own must find.
To determine if wise was spent the sands of time.

Paul Morabito ©

Jason P. Hein

Growing up on a secluded farm in the panhandle of Oklahoma, Jason P. Hein developed a unique point of view and literary sense as a young child. With few friends and little to entertain him, his imagination ran wild! With iconic names such as C.S Lewis and J.R.R Tolkien as literary inspirations, epic tales began to unfold inside the confines of his mind. These stories soon became the backbone for a rich fantasy land, now known as "The Varsian Kingdom."

As years and education expanded his mind, so they expanded the Kingdom of Varsia. With the launch of "The Varsian Kingdom Series" Jason is now offering his world for the exploration of intrigued minds and fantasy readers alike! Visit the Varsian Kingdom at VarsianKingdom.com

"A battle bought," tells the tragic tale of battle between countrymen and an invading force of dragons. It is unclear from the sketchy history just where this battle took place or who wrote it. What one can learn from these verses, however, is that victory comes with a great price.

8 A BATTLE BOUGHT

Crystal craters caress the tree line,
Smoke and smog arrest the sunshine.

Fiery flames frolic and prattle,
Formidable foes attest to battle.

Dead dragons defame the holly ground,
Wounded warriors nearly drowned.

Red rivers ruin the tree line,
Men mourning arrest the sunshine.

Victorious voices vanish from fields,
A battle bought with sword, life, and shield.

Jason P. Hein ©

Written by Braiden, founder of the "Rangers of the West" wrote this poem of his ancestors, the earth whisperers, who gave their life in the construction and defense of the great wall at Deanemis.

9 THE BUILDER'S TOMB

This wall so tall,
Will never fall.
It's stones are set,
Have not budged yet.

Beneath these bricks,
Lay bones and sticks.
Of fallen men,
Their tomb within.

May we seek,
Their life to keep.
For memory sake,
This walk I take.

To honor those,
Whom I emboss.
Who guard this land,
By their bricks that stand.

Jason P. Hein ©

This rare piece of poetry is dated to some one or two hundred years before The Great Scarring of the earth. Most records predating the scarring were destroyed. The author and prompt of this piece are unknown.

10 DRAGON SLAYER OF THE WEST

There was a Dragon, with a flagon,
The terror of the land.
The Dragon's plight was to fight,
None could before him stand.

There was a man from distant land,
Who sought to end his reign.
Despite great skill was weaker still,
Bereaved, he fled in pain.

There was a king with everything,
Until the Dragon's brew.
He sought the sum of the flagon's rum,
The contents which were true.

For in the east there was a beast,
The beast its name was "West."
And though the King sent everything,
The beast would kill his best.

So the Dragon, with the flagon,

Trekked to distant land.
And since his plight was to fight,
He before the beast did stand.

There was a fight, through day and night,
That shook the mountains down.
In the end the beast did bend,
And the Dragon took his crown.

The King he soared and would reward,
But Dragon wanted not, but rest.
So with a fame, the King gave name,
"Dragon, Slayer of the West."

Jason P. Hein ©

This song was written in 2379 AC. by Lady Goldwing on her first expedition to find the Hall of Fallen Heroes. As she sat beneath the willow trees where the Hatari river runs out of the northern Evilexose mountain range, she composed these words, later putting music to match.

11 SUMMER'S SONG

The trees, the breeze,
A gentle green.

See spring and sing,
In everything.

A bloom will loom,
On branches high.

From dead to red,
Against the sky.

The blossoms will, beauty spill,
A fragrant scent along.

Honey bees, in budding trees,
The sound of Summer's Song.

Jason P. Hein ©

This poem, written in 2383 AC. is attributed to the sixth specter of the Varsian Kingdom, Leila. It is said she wrote this poem after her death when the angel Shasia took her. Shasia allowed her to leave this piece in the Chronicles of Continuity as a legacy before continuing on to the world above.

12 A VOICE FROM THE PAST

When the past comes calling,
Whistling in your ear.
When your walls are falling,
Leaving exposed things so dear.

Don't bow your back,
To weight and strain.
Drift not back,
From whence you came!

When the pain's sweet voice,
Sings lullaby.
Though it sways your choice,
Though it tempts to try...

Let not your valor,
Wane to close.
Walk life's seashore,
Grow life's rose!

Take up your cross,
Daily strive.
Chisel off your dross,
For you are yet alive!

Jason P. Hein ©

(Excerpt from "Inspired Poetry" by Jason P. Hein)

13 SILVER MOON

The darkened sky looming by,
Stars shining in the sky.
A silver moon shining bright,
In the darkness of the night.

I sit above trees so tall,
Watching as my thoughts fall.
I sit on the cold hard ground,
Trees growing all around.

The light shining off the lake,
As I hold my heart to break.
Within my heart still pumps strong,
As I sing the sweetest song.

Reflections in the midnight,
Reflect the water's moonlight.
As silent ripples call me,
To break away and be free.

I'm floating out in blackness,
Surrounded by this darkness.
While looking at its greatness,
Staring from my faintness.

The dream of touching ground,
It's such a pleasant sound.
The trees growing green and tall,
The brown dirt cold in fall.

All a bitter memory,
Of my past's scenery.
Now it all has passed away,
In the darkness of the day.

Through the blackness now I fly,
As the moon floats on by.
I know it too will pass by soon,
As hands graze the silver moon.

The silver smooth shining bright,
In this everlasting night.
My reflection looking back,
An image set in black.

Reflecting rays of light,
Makes for such a stunning sight.
Stars reflecting in their place,
All around my smiling face.

I now with my finger trace,
While I'm floating out in space.
Across the surface turning,
It's wonders I am learning.

A land of silver pure,
Now of that I am sure.
Corrosions from the time faint,
Every now and then taint.

It's a work of God and art,
A shame we soon will part.
As the currents carry strong,
As they have for so long.

Slowly now I drift away,
After this pleasant day.
Other wonders this one mars,
That I've seen through the stars.

My muscles now stretching each,
As it slips out of reach.
To the stars I float away,
Currents pulling me astray.

Off to other sights to see,
As I float light and free.
I shall not forget this soon,
Remembering the silver moon.

Jason P. Hein ©

This particular rhyme was written by Biran Koru, son of the explorer Braden Koru, in the year 2010 AC. The story depicts the age old disagreement surrounding the ruins of Dolraeyoss. The town of Dolraeyoss was the largest and most prosperous town on earth before the Great Scarring occurred around 2000 AC. After the great scarring, the city was left in ruins. Years later when it was finally rediscovered approximately one hundred miles north of the Evilexose mountain range near the east end along the Sarengedeeze river, people began to say it was cursed. Others, in contrast, say it is in fact blessed because they believe it is where creation began. (Excerpt from "Poems of Varsian Lore" by Jason P. Hein)

14 THE RUINS OF DOLRAEYOSS

It's said they hold a curse,
The ruins of Dolraeyoss.
A barren land or worse,
Haunted by a ghost.

It's said the men who venture,
Into its crumbling midst.
Put themselves in danger,
By setting foot there where it sits.

It's said that in that sport,
The great scarring, it began.
Because wickedness was hot,
So was purged throughout the land.

Thus it's cursed they maintain,
From rock, to tree, to sand.
A desert place with little rain,
A barren lifeless land.

But others disagree,
There is no curse they say.
For if you venture in you'll be,
Blessed this very day.

It's not where scars were formed,
But where creation began.
And though by many they are scorned,
They hold fast in their stand.

Death and life in one place,
They both seem very close.
Make your choice, curse of grace,
In the ruins of Dolraeyoss.

Jason P. Hein ©

R.M. Romarney

R.M. Romarney was born and raised in a small mining town in the vast semi desert of central Australia where it seldom rains, towering dust storms blacken the sky, and a blazing sun blistered the skin. At age 21 he and his wife moved to the coastal city of Adelaide and started their family with the birth of two daughters.

He writes poetry in all styles and genres through the voices of many diverse characters. He believes his poems are not complete until he knows the deepest thoughts of the poem's protagonist, and he is in a love affair with the volta in stories, in poems and in song lyrics, the turning point of dramatic change in thought, emotion and circumstance.

15 THE SINGULAR CROSS

My burden breaks his feet
on old and well-worn cobble stones
and I am new and will be splendid
my life given to me by him
and I try and prepare to take his life.

Blood slowly drips from his head
but blood pours from the thorns
and I bled when I was felled
for I am the one.

Other trees symphonize with sympathy for me
turning their leaves away from the sun
but I will stand strong for him
bear his immeasurable weight show him that I care.

He carries me
and soon I will carry him
my bark stripped from me
could have shielded him from cast stones.

Please let me fall
hard upon the cobble stones
take his moment of rest
before the whips cut him to the bone again.

One nail pierces through his welcoming hand
a hand burdened with unending love
and the shattered nail braces and would not bend
as the nail cries for this man's hurt.

The hammer strikes a solid hit to make it swift
to not prolong this man's agony
and the hammer cries for this man
more strikes of malice to come.

And I ease the nails entry into me to soften the blow
and each progressing blow splinter me
and I cry as I soften the blows
for this is all I can do for him.

R.M. Romarney ©

16 SEVEN FEELINGS

Judas what did you feel
just seven feelings for you to kill
seven feelings then regret?

Give Jesus away with feelings
kill Jesus with feelings
in my mind
in my soul
seven feelings control.

Judas what did you feel
just seven feelings for you to kill?

God tell me now
am I too proud?

Judas I know what you feel
I feel
what you feel
seven feelings.

Your lust
for power over Jesus
Judas

your gluttony
all his prayers for you
Judas.

Your greed
all his holy thoughts for you
Judas.

Your sloth
you can't do, let him be who he is
Judas.

Your wrath
rage in you of his spiritual ways
Judas.

Your envy
of how he touches souls
Judas.

Your pride
for you, you must be better than he
Judas.

I feel
what you feel
seven feelings
then I feel your regret.

Judas you feel
just seven feelings for you to kill.

Kissed Jesus to High Priest
a certain death for him
love thief

to kill Jesus
you commit seven deadly sins.

I know your feelings Judas
your feelings are in me
just seven feelings that may
have killed Jesus on that day.

I feel
what you feel
seven feelings.

Then I feel your regret.

R.M. Romarney ©

17 WE WERE LONELY MY VALENTINE

Along a pavement of loneliness
you towards me
and I towards you
unknown celestial bodies eclipse at night.

We pass and our gravity of loneliness
brings us together
so close to touch
but not close enough.

Your presence draws my heart
and I feel you can't pull away
from gravity we stargaze
our loneliness orbits
and companionship to fill the black void.

We touch and our solitude
evaporates into the stratosphere
and the night is secluded
I take you as a lover
and you take me as yours
we enter the expanding universe at its core.

The night to linger in our arms
we feel humanity

as humans share
we need each other
as strangers share
we feel included and wanted
for one night only we are true lovers.

One last kiss my valentine
celestial bodies continue on their extraterrestrial journeys
as I walk in the breaking dawn
along the pavement of loneliness
I know loneliness can be confined.

R.M. Romarney ©

18 WASTED WORDS

If everyone gave wasted words
what would the words be?
solidarity
and words like that
harmony
another wasted word
togetherness
wasted words don't make a revolution.

I want to give the world wasted words
peace
and words like that
society
another wasted word
humanity
all just wasted words going nowhere.

Tell me your wasted words
singer singing a song
tweeter tweeting
written in your status
pen on paper to a hater
a greeting card to a friend
an actor's forgotten dialogue
a politician in a speech to a nation
teenagers saying more than their graffiti

poets creating a lost poem
a mother telling her newborn of all the things she can do.

Tell the world your wasted words
tenderness
companionship
here is my hand
give the world your wasted words.

A child's first words
when they say mummy or daddy
but really are saying the word
love
Have we all forgotten our first word?

If everyone gave wasted words
then one day the words wouldn't be wasted.

R.M. Romarney ©

19 THE PARADOX OF LOVE

I've seen how love makes people feel
and I want to feel.

It's like fire burning
or cold returning
it's like a stranger talking to you
or a lover loving you
it's like emotional healing
or with broken hearts dealing.

It's like you are running
for absolutely nothing
it's like living or dying
laughing then crying
it's like lover become hater
destroyer then reconciliator
it's like the future in your head
your lover dies
your future is now dead.

It's how love makes you feel
overwhelming your senses
breaking down your defences.

I have seen the paradox of love

and I know it will be
an impending tragedy for you and me.

R.M. Romarney ©

20 BLUE PLANET PHENOMENON

She's from the pink planet called Constellation
he's from the dark planet beyond
under a constant monitor
no love a interplanetary phenomenon.

He's an interstellar
she's studying astronomy
what they have seen sets in motion their biology
they will meet on the blue planet
they should know better
it's death if they get together.

Interplanetary love is forbidden
their passion keep it hidden
they should know better
but they must be together
to the blue planet
love velocity interstellar.

Crossing Earth's longitudes
hiding their love in the new year's eve multitudes
they should know better
their love still not allowed
under another planets blanketing cloud.

Planet Earth in unified love
new year's eve blue planet phenomenon
she will fall pregnant
their baby conceived at a time of human unity
their unborn baby and united humanity
become one in harmony.

Interstellar before they're discovered
too late their love uncovered
they should know better
it's death for forbidden love together.

Trial on dark planet
they will all die today
"Kill them now"
judgment say.

They plea for their unborn baby's mercy
a reprieve
child leniency
only for their baby clemency.

"Bring on the birth" authorities say
a unpredicted baby delivery
conceived in a time of human unity
a love descendant of humanity.

Interstellar love racing
interplanetary embracing
human love emanating
from their newborn baby
blanketing pink planet with love
blanketing dark planet with love.

Two planets authority depleting

two planets a love meeting
now love not forbidden
love never to be hidden
interstellar love plea
she and he with their baby to go free.

R.M. Romarney ©

Irum Zahra

Psychaotic is Irum Zahra's first of many books.
She believes in recognition rather than money and fame. Her
idea of happiness is inner peace and nothing else, because at
the end, you're the person you have to live and die with.
Writing is her anchor to all the hurt in the world and she will
continue to write till her soul leaves this earth.

Facebook:
https://www.facebook.com/BeyondTheEdgeOfSanity

21 PRIZE POSSESSION

Let's go for a walk
In those dark caves
I'll show you where
I'll keep you safe
Locked in a silver coffin
Carved with my poetry for you
Waiting to be occupied
And when the moon rises
Behind those clouds
I'll let you out to see me
The only vision of beauty
For your eyes only
I'll soothe your neck
And let it bleed a bit
I have a theory
That maybe your blood
Imitates my favorite perfume
And I would like to wear you now.

Irum Zahra ©

22 THE CROSSROADS

It was shady and cold
Like a horror story being told
I felt the winds change their course
Turning all the pages of my book at once
There and then I stared
At the dark shadow
Standing before me
With eyes red as hell
I could hear him whisper
In the tone of wrath and anger
Yet so inviting
Like some old perfume's scent
The devil told me
To meet him at the crossroads
I listened and my heart pounded
I'll kiss the luck in your life
And make the fate fall in love with you
I will show you all the ways
You can come undone
I will grant all your wishes
Revenge and love
I'll show you the pleasure in pain and torture
I'll show you the beauty in scars
I listened and stood still
I paused as the world slipped away
And I followed him.

Irum Zahra ©

23 TAINTED

Have you seen a rose?
So pure, so pretty
Untouched and blood red
But have you seen it burn?
Watch it turn to ashes?
I like the unusual things
Like the burning cigarette
Absorbing in my blood
Turning my lungs black
My own chosen poison
Have you seen someone smoke?
Some get intrigued
Others turn around in disgust
Have you ever asked?
How the blood red
Turned dark?
Did you ever see?
How the purity turned tainted?
Did you see my heart?
Which isn't untouched anymore?

Irum Zahra ©

24 SOMEWHERE IN THE GRAVEYARD

Stillness
Sings in the graveyard
The trees
The winds
People
All still.
Waiting for an accident,
By us
By our actions
Maybe we'll dig them all up
Since we're so fascinated
By the dead
Than the living
With their stories
Than our own.

Irum Zahra ©

25 THE ALTERNATE LOVE

If only you could feel
How proud her eyes were
They could turn down a king
And bring him to his knees
An ego so high
Mountains would feel like stones
If only she would let me strangle her
With love and devotion
She would like a black stone necklace
I would push a pillow to her face
And own her breaths
I would hit her face so hard
I know she loves scars on herself
I would erase all her past
And her mind numb
Then I'll write my own
Paralyzing story,
On the pages she holds so dear.

Irum Zahra ©

Regis McCafferty

Regis McCafferty, is the author of numerous articles, short stories, and four novels. A recognized poet, he is a member of the Canton Writer's Guild, writes a regular poetry column for their monthly newsletter, and is also a member of The Academy of American Poets. His first volume of collected poems, *Another View From The Park*, was published while living in New Mexico. He has recently relocated to Northern Ohio.

He has been writing poetry, novels and short stories for many years, and in 1993, 1994, and 1995, he was honored to serve as a poetry judge for the Columbus Ohio Arts Council. His latest novel, *The Nude on the Cigarette Case*, was named a Finalist in the Mystery category by the 2014 Next Generation Book Awards committee. He is currently working on a sequel to that novel, and a second poetry collection.

26 TWEED

I.

The tweed jacket hung on his bony frame
as if on a wooden hanger; slightly
higher in the back than in front and bowed
forward, misshapen and loose. Pockets bulged
with things of old men: Several matchbooks, mints,
and a soft tobacco pouch in the left -
Two cheek-oiled pipes stuck out from the right;
the wool permanently stretched to fit them.

He checked his pocket watch and finding he
had ten minutes till the next bus, reached in
his pocket for a pipe. His hand found one,
but a finger found a burn hole as well
and he paused, three fingers around the pipe
and his middle finger stuffed through the hole.

II.

The finger gave an upside down salute
to the bag lady standing next to him.
She was looking at him. No smile, no frown,
just looking. He smiled. She looked. He frowned.
She looked. He turned his hand in his pocket
to adjust the salute proper side up
and wiggled his finger at her. "Bastard,"
she said. He shrugged his shoulders, then turned

to walk, with broad grin, to the next bus stop.

He lifted a pipe from his pocket,
tamped the plug in the bowl with his finger
and put a match to it, still grinning at
the thought of the startled "bag" behind him.
Sometimes life gives us simple things, he thought -
You made my day Honey, and I made yours.

Regis McCafferty ©2000

27 HAPPY FACE

February, nineteen ninety seven.
I was headed south on the interstate
when a rusty Ford van slowly passed by.
I didn't pay much attention till
I saw the happy face on the back door.
It had only one eye… in the center of its forehead.
The neat printing above it said,
"Happy Mutants For Nuclear Energy".
That piqued my interest!
As I increased my speed and pulled closer,
I read on the side, "Save The Planet,"
each letter a different color.
There were two young women inside,
a blonde driving, with a brunette as co-pilot,
her sandaled feet propped on the dash.

And suddenly, it was many years ago.
We sat in a smoky little coffee shop
just shy of a sprawling college campus
getting high on espresso.
She was dishwater blonde and would have driven
a daisy covered Volkswagon if she had one.
As it was, she barely had bus fare,
so she walked. It kept her body tight.
I liked that. Stairs led from the outside

to her small third floor flat.
Hot summers. Cold winters.
Opposite her bed was a large window,
and I could watch the moon slip over the window sill
as it crept upward toward faded wallpaper.
She couldn't see it... She was on top.

Regis McCafferty ©2000

28 HE SAT THE SADDLE LOOSE

(A story of Gill Colorado 1880s)

He sat his saddle loose,
his body whipcord lean,
his Bisley Colt in crossdraw style,
his face not soft, nor mean.

The sun and wind and sand,
etched Arroyos on his face -
His Stetson making shadows,
brim down and low in place.

He nudged his appaloosa
to a gentle walk down hill,
the morning sun behind him
as he made the town of Gill.

The main street was deserted,
except for one lone man –
His name was Chester Martin,
a gun from Johnson's clan.

He reined the appaloosa,
at the Texas Jack saloon,
dismounted slow, and eyed the man,
each waiting on their doom.

Neither spoke, just stood apart,
'bout thirty feet or so,
as if waiting on a signal –
some sign they both would know.

The hand of Johnson's man
moved slightly toward his hip –
But the Bisley hand was quicker,
and his shot cracked like a whip.

The Johnson's man, suspended,
not dead, but not alive,
slowly crumpled to the street…
then stared with lifeless eyes.

The Bisley Colt returned
to his holster like a ghost,
as the lean man slowly shuffled
to the wind worn hitching post.

He mounted appaloosa,
turned from the Texas Jack,
then rode around the body,
the sun still at his back.

He sat his saddle loose,
his body whipcord lean,
his Bisley Colt in crossdraw style,
his face not soft, nor mean.

Regis McCafferty ©2012

29 COLLEEN

She has a ribbon in her hair.
Lime green, I think, and velvet; loosely tied,
as if some subtle dare would tumble it
from all the softness hidden there.
I wonder.... Even if I tried
to touch gently, softly, as the spirit
of a breeze might unaware, caress the sea,
Would she not know that it was I?

Such innocence would love permit
so soft a gesture, as to her would be
a moonbeam falling softly across her face.
And in the hush of night as would befit
a child's dreams of kindred love and grace,
I brush her tresses gently back in place.

Regis McCafferty ©1996

30 TO APPLESAUCE

The yellow truck arrived one morn,
and what I saw, I could have sworn,
took me by surprise. The apple tree
that graced my yard, that canopy
that nurtured me with shade and fruit,
was trimmed so close I thought the root
would surely die. And yet this year,
to my delight, with Autumn near,
my little tree had done me proud.
I laughed a hearty laugh aloud!
To applesauce, the tree was trimmed,
yet sprouted apples limb to limb.

Regis McCafferty ©1995

31 CARDBOARD BOX

The whistle blew long and loud and lonely -
Echoed through the underpass to break up
on the trestle that crossed the river.

He sat in his cardboard box,
turned sideways against the wind.
Moving, he shoveled his ass tighter into the
corner as he pulled the wool blanket
close around his legs.

He wanted to leave his shoes on,
but if he drank the bottle of Port
held close inside his coat, he'd black out ...
Then some bastard would steal his shoes
from his feet while he slept.

He inched the bottle up, and cracked the seal ...

The whistle blew long and loud and lonely -
piercing frigid air and cardboard box,
as the Diesel rolled and shook the ground.

He sat in his cardboard box,
now covered with ice and snow,
his bare feet drifted over,
their form lost in white,

eyes open, empty, staring at the endless track.

Regis McCafferty ©2000

32 THE MOUNTAIN

I am somehow in tune with the mountain,
in tune, but not comfortable.
There is always an edginess,
awareness that my humanity is out of place.

The mountain is hard, granite hard,
notwithstanding a bed of pine needles,
oak, maple, or aspen leaves.
Hard even under thick, multihued moss.

The mountain has its own way;
it tolerates myriad creatures that crawl
across its surface, creep through
its forests and brush below the tree-line.

Bear, deer, lynx, cougar, fox, squirrel,
other animals and millions of insects
inhabit its skin. Some are transient
like humans, some not. Coyotes.

Something shadows me as I walk
the narrow path along the cliff face.
Coyote? Perhaps, but more likely

my own fear of the unknown that waits.

Fear is patient, much like the mountain
that sustains life through forbearance.
Fear endures, hovers, surrounds –
Like the coyote . . . Hungry … Waiting.

Regis McCafferty ©2012

Roberto Carlos Martinez

Roberto Carlos Martinez is a Salvadorian-born American author. He is the author of four works of poetry: The Blue-Eyed Monster Dragged Me into Love, Imperfection in a Perfect World, Dreaming Outside of Destiny, and Inconsolable. He has a B.A. in Psychology and is currently obtaining his M.Ed. at George Mason University.

His confessional poetry has focused on improving perceptions of death, depression, kindness, love, and spirituality.

33 DREAMS

We will seek dreams
things we can only see inside of us
but have not yet touched.

Dreams that give way to other dreams.
But the most dangerous dreams are those that are not our
own.

We clench onto them the way the ones who created them
clench to us.
With time our own dreams begin to disappear
and so does a part of our soul.

But the most dangerous dreams are those that are not our
own.
For they seek approval and acknowledgement from another
dreamer.
We cannot dream for another, but we can approve and
acknowledge our own dreams.

Roberto Carlos Martinez ©

34 THE PATH OF LOVE

I remember the first time my mother said, "I love you."
Although I did not know the context of her "love"
I knew it meant something.

Then there was the first time I said, "I love you" to my first
love.
I thought it was love, but it lacked a planted seed and it lacked
nourishment.
There was a quick snap,
a connection,
but there was nothing holding it together.

There was the first time I said, "I love you" to the one I would
eventually marry.
I quickly thought it was love, but I learned that love has to be
built gently piece by piece.
Many cannot master this puzzle from the outside.

It's not created in a week, or a month, or a year.
You come together and a seed is created.
One day we created our own puzzle.

From there grows your love and you nourish it
with positive words and affirming actions.
One day that love becomes whole and holds itself together.
A love that is soft, gentle, and malleable.
Yet you know that one day, it will all fall away

but love is so strong that even in its simplest form it will always exist.

Roberto Carlos Martinez ©

35 CHANGES

Too long we ignore the emotional abuse.
The pain that doesn't heal
that haunts you in your sleep
that silently awakens and drags you through the ancient sand.

I was guilty too
taking for granted the damage that had been done.
As the inner scars healed I started forgetting.

I gently lifted myself from the pain.
You did too.

Roberto Carlos Martinez ©

36 THE BEAST

It lies dormant
you always know it is there
but you try not to sympathize with it.

It extends its long white wings over your shoulders
the right wing caressing your left shoulder
you pretend not to notice
as its tired breathing
echoes through you.

But one day something wakes up in you again
you look back once again.
Its breathing becomes words once again
its wings become empathy.

The burning memories
the sleepless nights
the cold tears
the bloody knife
and the thoughts of ending.

But there is another figure in the room
it places its left hand over your right shoulder
its breathing becomes words
its hand becomes sympathy.

"Everything is okay," the figure whispers.

Roberto Carlos Martinez ©

37 EMPIRE OF DIRT

There were those times you hurt someone I loved.
You used the sharpness of your words to cut deeply
making my loved one bleed over and over again.
I heard the quick trickling sound of the red blood.

I learned to watch from afar.
In the silence I would calculate my every move.
Many did underestimate me
it was their way of feeling strong.

For so long you felt like a queen.
but to feel it was not enough.
There were many games you said to yourself in your head.

Many games you did play
but your materialistic kingdom came down
I heard the sharp scraping sound of its quick fall.
All the crosses could not hold the weight of karma.

Afterwards,
I felt dirty for playing the game.

Roberto Carlos Martinez ©

38 THE HUMAN EXPERIENCE

Maybe there are no secrets
there is nothing to discover
just places and spiritual beings to experience.

Sometimes we are like children
sitting on the green grass and looking ahead pondering the
mysteries of life
waiting for the answers.

The silhouettes dance gracefully within us
tempting us to take chances.

In self-reflection we realize
we are interconnected
together with many.

Maybe there are no secrets.
There is nothing to discover
just places and spiritual beings to experience.

Roberto Carlos Martinez ©

David Russell

b. 1940. Resident in the UK. Writer of poetry, literary criticism, speculative fiction and romance. Main poetry collection *Prickling Counterpoints* (1998); poems published in online *International Times*. Main speculative works *High Wired On* (2002); *Rock Bottom* (2005). Translation of Spanish epic *La Araucana*, Amazon 2013. Romances: *Self's Blossom; Explorations; Further Explorations; Therapy Rapture; Darlene, An Ecstatic Rendezvous* (all pub Extasy (Devine Destinies). Singer-songwriter/guitarist. Main CD albums *Bacteria Shrapnel* and *Kaleidoscope Concentrate*. Many tracks on You Tube, under 'Dave Russell'

39 THE FIRST ADVENTURE

That shadowy entrance, subdued glint,
spark of eyes!
You trod all cultures with your classic grace
Of posture, figure, profile
The breathy touch, so tentative,
The answering squeeze
All beams and tiptoes as we trod
Unspoken message:
"The dream's come true"

The curtain nearly volunteered
To close itself.
I was poised to give the word;
Fired by our kisses, you took it from my
mouth

Each garment spoke surrender as it fell
A flower-show of fabrics
Adoring those limbs which they had covered;
Warm air on new divested skin
Near liquid in its heady density

Our bodies new-revealed, dreamed up
A gallery of art-figures,
Our mounting breath

Kindled their animation in our honour
Those facing entities suffused with mutual
nourishment

The rising sun the backcloth of our dual climax
The bathing epilogue
The farewell walk
A froth of blossom round our tender steps
That fleeting perfection was the purest art
Framed in an idyllic memory.

David Russell ©

40 POWER KERNELS

Break down the elements, split them
To non-existence;
Then shatter all solidity's illusions,
Free impulses
Beyond the viscous mind, still feeling hard
By vanity's gas upholstered.

And then, for happiness's definition,
Shut the door;
Relax, and don't be squeamish;
For every grit of teeth, a pull of trigger,
A sear, a cloud…

Then, if the bacillus, the charge
Breaks through even your filter-screen,
Then paper barrier that defines
Your victims and yourselves…

And you, amoebae, become specimens
Now that your brainchild ogres
Have outstepped the frames of will;

Oh super-brains! Limp, flapping squids;
Now that you've burst your cranial canisters,
Now that you've blundered on the combination
To open up the vault

Wherein you case your muffled
Conscience-bleats
to soothing, doped oblivion;

Did you first conquer all remorse, all fear,
Destroy all that might have the power to save?

And will you now be laid low, by yourselves,
Even denied all retribution's flames,
All instantaneous dignity?

Oh ones still solid, cynicism's crust
Thickens and stifles, yet absorbs,
Driving life's final spark to desperation;
No scope to flash
Without full-voiding all outside itself.

Oh loosen now your halters,
Clean growth, no fission-cancers,
Live now; be novae.

David Russell ©

41 CHECKPOINT

Lurching, they bluster – ghouls into the chasm.

Fierce lava, blowing, nullifies their fall
And dissipates harsh gravity's concussion,
Forces a seething screen of phoenix cowardice,
Leaping to swell
Into a fresh, mendacious crust,
Tripping and throttling the led
Into a smear upon pure metamorphic beauty.

The skeleton's jaws yawn apart;
A stranded mountaineer was frozen
At his prime pinnacle,
Denied warm, compromised decay;
A calcium landmark now, but broken loose;
A boulder never neutral
To those in fear.

One gouged and bored –
New Sisyphus, with ever-sinking aspiration
For no stress, no fall –
For him the indefatigable light
Breathes limbo silicosis.

Can they combine? Eternity transcends the cheap ideal
Of mutual obliteration.

A mountaineer trapped in a submarine,
A miner in a satellite,
A megalomaniac performing his own precious lobotomy
Hoping the abolished question mark
Can keep things safe and solid.

Purgation's smudged when bound to fire,
Denied release from fizzy process,
And even air can clog and sludge
The ultimate suction of life's syllables
Into fatuous pinprick stars,

No line can break full circle.

David Russell ©

42 TROPIC ENCOUNTER

Off a veranda runway
We wafted to euphoria
On wine's, acacias' nectar
Through sweet hypnosis,
Novelty, coy smiles – a mystery
Enhanced by blithe uncertainty;
Our smiles affirmed fresh questions,
Then tuned new swaying, swirling,
Now melting all cold purposes –
Two forms, one tide, one breeze.
Soft touch on satin, linen,
Crisp fashions hiding, hinting,
Soft rhythms cleaving;
Dance swinging into pirouette –
Your gown and petticoat as wave crests,
Clouds, suspending gravity –
Fresh beauty cleared;
Dance lifting into dress's falling,
Swathes beneath blooms' wholeness lying,
Bodies rising to depths' call.
The warm lagoon, us all embracing
Drew us through currents, eddies, wakes
To polyps' bower.
Love's lull, love's breeze, love's gale,
Love's lightning whirlpool
Made us into our element,
Made us monsoon abandonment;

Love's flotsam, now surviving
We forebore
To drown in high perfection,
But salvaged driftwood memories;
Salvaged ourselves
As sea-shells, coral flower-shapes
Happy shelved.

David Russell ©

43 IMMORTALITY

You carried your vengeance beyond decease –
Slowed down the pyre's cleansing,
Slowed down the soil's, the water's warmth,
Left total body change open to the senses –
Pursued your cause beyond its effects,
Stepped out beyond all examples,
Further than all reflections,
Forestalled all worth –
All kindred, all common links –

Seeking to frame a cleansing,
Seeking a bubbling stench,
Blinding off the cause, sinking the bubble,
Aerating the stench.

Since you thought that such a front
Would keep your footsteps light,
Sidestep the quicksand's dam
So that you could token-touch a cairn –
Erected but unentered,
Tactile – taking an unbroken course –
Blinded wholly on touching.

The given whole, from oneself all taken –
The river whole, clean-bleached,
Its bed eroded;
Nodding answers from the straight,

The cogged, the balanced;
Pressing blinks for engulfment
From the all –

The all whole, harnessed,
Blasted, made permanent:
Some lichen fossilized
Inside a flagstone.

Sad lump beyond your strength,
Your total celebration –
Sunken, dreaded – an iceberg's reality;
Prismatic, pricking some seeming velvet womb
That rips the skin when touching it;
Total cold, some shivering rib-case
At last replaceable, to thread and string
The lesser wonders.

Total colour, total glittering –
In nothing lacking save the power
To follow one another.

Headlong longing, and yet not in for pitching without;
A limb for pitching, unditched by gravity,
For wishing, jumping.

Mere within the drowning,
Jumping mere with burning.

David Russell ©

44 BURGLARS OF BRITAIN

Here's good luck to the Burglars of Britain
The Underworld Securicor;
For burglars in worthy disguises
Will keep the wolf from your door.

If you read in your papers
You may recollect
Poor deviant victims
Of callous neglect;
It's just through sheer luck
You've kept your self-respect.

But you're safe, you're safe,
You're safe – aye; you're safe.
Go crack a safe with the Burglars of Britain,
The salt of old Albion's land.

It's only through them
That you're where you are now;
So go rest contented,
Don't ask why or how.
Just let them go freely,
To plunder and roam;
They'll cushion your country,
Your comfort, your home,

And you're safe, you're safe,
You're safe – aye; you're safe.
Go crack a safe with the Burglars of Britain,
The salt of old Albion's land.

Through VAT and Income Tax
You meet the expense
Of a bad rip-off budget
And bogus defence;
You keep your mouths shut,
Four you cannot make sense

You feel safe, you're safe,
You're safe – aye; you're safe.
Go crack a safe with the Burglars of Britain,
The salt of old Albion's land.

Those generous donators
Of money reward,
They're deep into graft
And they're well into fraud;
They ravage the earth
Just to keep you dead bored.
You lose everything
But you're not overawed
When everything's comprehensively insured
And the law of the jungle says
Who shall be gored.

And you're safe, you're safe,
You're safe – aye; you're safe.
Go crack a safe with the Burglars of Britain,
The salt of old Albion's land.

You draw up the shield

Of a great company
A big crowbar crossed
By a skeleton key;
You're happy as slaves
'Cos you think that you're free

And you're safe, you're safe,
You're safe – aye; you're safe.
Go crack a safe with the Burglars of Britain,
The salt of old Albion's land.

Get off that soapbox,
Stop thumping that tub;
Go straight to the Mafia
And pay them your sub.
The world does you right
If you join in the club

And you're safe, you're safe,
You're safe – aye; you're safe.
Go crack a safe with the Burglars of Britain,
The salt of old Albion's land.

It's only through them
That you're where you are now;
So go rest contented,
Don't ask why or how.
Just let them go freely,
To plunder and roam;
They'll cushion your country,
Your comfort, your home,

And you're safe, you're safe,
You're safe – aye; you're safe.
Go crack a safe with the Burglars of Britain,

The salt of old Albion's land.

David Russell ©

45 CREMATION

I've always believed in cremation;
Flames bleach the world, unclutter living things.

Let scum survivors, grasshoppers
Leave cemeteries a mess
Of living impulses dismembered.
Not knowing fire's totality
But sickly honouring it stunting
In tortured carbon stench.

I've always believed in cremation
Ever since I read of great skull mountains;
Those potash handfuls are so clean –
A powdered love of life.

I think of bones and masonry,
Of skeletons and architects.
Humanity's erections;
Are we the greater polyps?
No – we are parasites.

No longer do we draw from deserts
Our pride's stark affirmation
But – aimless – puncture, scar and crater
Real skin, flesh, sinew, bone.

Prime tombs remain, aimed starwards,

Steering earth;
For ones they were, for everyone.
Termite-wretches, harsh-bound inside one frame
With all for others.

So is this past? Are we now free –
With monuments so empty, blinded to stars,
Time-choked, chasing a mercury present –
That wriggling lump we would congeal
To parry our mortality –
Reassured joke, bluff, never using
By thinking of dismantling
When Fury, justly channeled,
Skims from eccentric earth?

The first was built to say
"We stand forever, cleaving heaven and earth."

The last: "We can accept the moment only;
When all's affirmed, we are as powder."

I've always believed in cremation.

David Russell ©

Mallory Smart

Mallory Smart is an American fiction-writer and poet from Chicago.

She was born on September 11, 1990 and at the young age of 23, became the founder of the transgressive new publishing company, Maudlin House.

The author of the existential poetic nightmare, Fear Like A Habit, Smart spends her days lost in her own mind traveling and fearing death.

There are many more works to come...

46 CALL OF THE VOID

Eras spent adrift,
Parked in cars and one-way careers.
Headlight authorities stare down from across the way,
But I still feel alone against the judgment.
Latterly holding tribute for weeds and the misguided fruits of toil.
The corporate playground proud,
without any trees.
A mere leviathan structure minus some leaves.
Concede the will of the name.
Oh, how they yield to the road that they must travel!

Might such a void subside?
Could all the colleges of the world ever fulfill it?
Or are we but a vacuum for hunger and defeat.
The pain of a nation carried in unlit compartments–
Buried somewhere between mothballs,
And Obama's change.
Drenched in the mirage of civilization.
Searching for a place called home,
Yet always adrift in a trench called soul and mind.
A battle waged amid hope and respite.
Hurting for something more,
Willing to die for life.

Mallory Smart ©

47 ONE TIME I TOOK AMBIEN AND NOTHING HAPPENED...

Every harvest moon, if it wasn't weird,
I'd crawl below your covers
and camp beside your legs.
And the legs would remind me of life
and indifference from when I was a child.
Everyone knows the best way you can ever feel
is ever, if at all.
Every morning we would make neither love,
nor war, but coffee.
Neither would change things
But I still need a fix.
And then maybe I can try.
I'd whisper poetry under covers with bated breath
to the sorrow of this broken sphere
into the night,
until the lamps went out
and you'd go to sleep.
But I don't know what it's like to sleep anymore.
I only know how to dream…

Mallory Smart ©

48 HITCHHIKING WITH A BROKEN THUMB

Meandering down broken road,
the man defies the night.
Tightrope on edge,
nothingness is more,
flesh and bone
waiting on breath.
His shattered body has no recall.
The eye surrounds him,
it is the window to his soul.
Dark and squalid.
He is dreariness every day.
Rows of incandescent lights expose
his being to the world
like defiled motel rooms
and transvestite lounge.
Passing immorally soaked cars,
hugging roadside shoulders
He is the unwelcomed,
unwanted bastard of us–
Cry to the road,
and plead to society.
Tainted the flesh of skid marks,
and excess.

still his lifeless body,
endures this cursed wait.
Endless night,

to priceless dawn.
He tramps among us,
a vestige.
Headed everywhere.
but going nowhere.

Mallory Smart ©

49 BLANKS AND BANTER

My mind often blanks with words and ideas
And unfinished texts.

I have visions of Christine Baranski in a seat
with her head cocked back
laughing and I don't know why…
I many times wonder about the meaningless in life
and why anyone should bother doing anything.

Hedonism makes so much more sense once you realize God is
dead and you will be too.

Haunted by the allure of fame,
guilted by my need for validation.

I want to be a great artist but want is almost never enough.

I'm not sure what it even means to be great.

I have considered making a tumblr blog, because someday
someone might want to see the roots to all my ideas.

But then I lie awake wondering why anyone would want to
see mine as opposed to someone else's.
I'm not better than the next writer.
But I'd like to be.

But I'm not trying to be competitive,
I'm a communist...
But I should like to feel that someone thought my thoughts
meant something.

God knows I don't...

It has become increasingly obvious to me that in our world of
intangibility, thoughts are the world's most valuable
commodity (ahead of mcdonalds, sex, and warfare).

That being said...

I need new yoga pants.

Mallory Smart ©

49 WISDOM TOOTHED WORDS

In the words of a generation of the apathetic,
the words you wake up to after a drunk misadventure,
the words a bum uses as kindling and never could absorb,
the words of how, and
the words of never-was:
"BE HERE" and "BE NOW"
just because…

Mallory Smart ©

Carolyn O'Connell

Carolyn lives in London, England and works with local groups. Her poems have been published in the English magazines Envoi, Interpreter's' House, Aireings among others and by the Celebrating Adlestrop Poetry Society. They have also been published in online magazines and anthologies. Her poems have been translated and broadcast into Romanian through the Translation Project. She is listed on poetrypf.com and is a member of the UK Poetry Society.

50 DETECTING WINGS

Over opaque leaves where blue spikes bloomed
wings spread silk threads spinning light
as air swirls dreadlocked mist down
roofs, paths, roads, twisted trees, pale lamplights.

Expectant windows whisper lighted promise
spiders unroll nets of flowing light
over softly shrouded houses
clothing children's sleep with hopes, ploys,

forged as from plangent silver struck, wrought
to filigree, chalice cups or even icon wings:
from skilled fingers sensitive to the metal's
ever changing song beneath hammer, fire, forge.

Retelling angels of Greek Byzantium their silver wings
enfolding ancient faces lost in age
beneath effacing plaster, rubble,
twisting time, faith, within the folds of feuding empires.

Mist deepens measuring night's clock
bending the fragile wings they lift
as if a mother's finger smoothed
the hair of her dreaming child - inscribing care.

Carolyn O'Connell ©

51 21st CENTURY CHRISTMAS – THE TREE

Setting out to buy a Christmas tree
on Christmas Eve the shops sold out.
No trees in markets, stalls had gone
there wasn't even one at all?

We trekked to forest but no luck
only black branches greeted us,
no conifers rose clothed in green
where would we get a Christmas tree?

Too late to get a feigned tall fir
online, too late for Amazon
no drone to drop outside the door
desired decorated tree -
they still rely on carriers.

How can we follow Albert's dictum
find traditional tree, fill the picture
of festive family grouped around
a fancy spruce or pristine pine.

In 1850 it was perfectly possible
to buy a tree on Christmas Eve
or as told in "A Christmas Carol"
that day a goose for family feast

but what the Dickens its 2013

they're ordered online in November
celebrated Black Friday bargains
so on Christmas eve we'll have to settle
for a Christmas tree as a 3D printout.

Carolyn O'Connell
© December 2013

52 ELEMENTS

1. Water.

You are the sculptor taking your chisel
carving rock, coastline, and mountain
scattering pebbles forming sand.

You reshape, reform our structures
into new gods whose faces
shine in the mirrors you strew
over our towns, fields, harbours.

We recoil from your strength
but need your essence for life.

2. Wind.

You are the hammer striking the chisel
powered by the sculptor's vision the energy
of his desire, moulder of his dreams.

You invade our spaces; disturb our minds
with the muscle of your talent
our structures pale and fall before your skill
you are the creator, the destroyer.

3 Fire.

You are the engine of the sculptor's forge
igniting creativity, edging his chisel
to a honed blade ready to etch new forms.

You uplift the oceans; reform islands
resurface the land with new soil, redirect rivers
extract where fertility emerges.

4. Earth.

You are the marble of our existence
holding the elements in your orbit.
Water clothes you in a velvet robe
nurturing life. Wind breathes filling
our lungs with flavours as fire's
eminence swells and wanes.

Carolyn O'Connell ©

53 AFTER THE STORMS

The waters have receded, wind softened
the sky holds warmth in its colours
blue has replaced constant grey
as winter relaxes its binding grasp.

Defying the detoxification of flooding
ruined crops, muddied cows
water's realignment of towns
storm manipulation of coastline

snowdrops sugar the garden
crocus embroidery lawns, banks
their rich silks subtle with promise
engaging eye, mind and nose

as hellebores nod darkly at
daffodils damply chiding showers
into rainbows dipping into
shadows lurking promise

of future days when they are
sought for relief in heat.
A heat we welcome as the
land warms.

Carolyn O'Connell ©

54 ANSWERING THE CHALLENGE

Thrown by a withered hand
a slick of hate pollutes the world
its net enslaves the innocent
rape, death and silence is its goal.

The face belonging to the hand
remains hidden while the young die,
seduced by promises of eternal life
their bodies wrecked by hate's shrapnel.

This Ebola of the mind corrupts - its spores
reshaping faith, culture to its cause;
rejecting those who give their all
to bring health, happiness, joy and empathy.

Fighting for an omnipotent Creator,
who needs no man's defence
and holy men who sleep in peace;
seduced by hate they crave love.

Love is the boom to throw upon
the writhing sea-storm; it catches
the slick. Roll in the net, repair
and clean with prayer and love.

Carolyn O'Connell ©

Carolyn has a collection "Timelines" published by Indigo dreams.

Frederick Espiritu

Frederick Espiritu is a telecom engineer-turned-entrepreneur after founding Friggies, a social enterprise based in the Philippines that is committed to making the world a healthier and better place through its products and services.

He believes that changing the world begins with oneself. Instead of digesting business books, he dwells more reading about spirituality, ancient wisdom and philosophy for personal growth. As he transcends, the Inner Poet in him has also come alive. He considers Bible passages among the great writings and Rumi, the mystic Sufi as his greatest influence.

Fred's poems mostly come out spontaneously as reflection of his life experiences. Simple yet profound, his poetry revolves around the beauty of the heart, which is Love.

55 A LETTER TO THE BELOVED

Let me love you, until you fall in love with yourself.
Let my light burn for you, until you feel the warmth of your
own flame.
Let me sing, until you can hear your music.
My Beloved, for as long as you are dreaming
let me stay awake,
until you, my true Love, are no longer asleep.

Frederick Espiritu ©

56 YOUR HOME IS IN YOUR HEART

Open your doors.
Welcome all visitors.
Fear, Anger, Grief and their relatives
Let them in.

Greet them with a smile.
Ask where did they come from,
And what stories they bring.
Listen.
They will get tired speaking.

When they become hungry,
Do not feed them.
When they become thirsty,
Pour them wine until they're drunk.
Give them a hug and whisper,
"You've come to the wrong place.
Go and Peace be with you."

Breathe. Today is through.
Sleep. Tomorrow is the beginning of your journey.

Darkness awaits outside.
Carry the light and keep it burning.
Every wanderer you meet is searching for a star.
Be the Sun, and shine without asking.

Then, keep walking.

Once in a while, be still.
Look around and witness every miracle.
If in your path you lose sight,
Close your eyes
And you will remember your way back home.

Frederick Espiritu ©

57 LIFE'S A FRIEND

If you befriend fear,
what else is there to be afraid of?

If you befriend pain,
what else is there to suffer from?

If you befriend the past,
what else is there to regret about?

If you befriend your enemy,
who else is there to fight?

My friend, life is not a battle.

If there is no more fighting,
All that is left is the beauty
That remains to be seen.
Love.

Frederick Espiritu ©

58 LOST AND FOUND

Separate but one,
Broken but whole.
This is where I find solitude.

You are because I am,
I am because you are.
This is where I find solace.

You are asleep,
I am awake.
We are lost in a dream.
This is the place where we meet.

Frederick Espiritu ©

59 GRATITUDE

Right here, right now, at this very moment,

I am grateful not for the music I am hearing,

but for the gift of hearing the music.

I am grateful not for the words I am speaking,

but for the gift of speaking the words.

I am grateful not for the emotion I am feeling,

but for the gift of feeling the emotion.

In Love.

I am grateful because I am.

Frederick Espiritu ©

Mark Green

Married with two children and born in Lichfield, Staffordshire.

Started writing just before the millennium around 1998 whereupon I wrote my first poem and sent it to the Daily Mail poet of the year competition. I received runner upper award, £50 cheque and a free book of the "Nations Favourite Poems." The poem that I entered was called 'You' and features in my book "Rhymes from the Book of Life."

After writing the poem, I started dabbling in writing a novel, which was going well until I had a bottle of wine (estimated quantity) one night and accidentally deleted the file, with no back up. The book was about 50,000 words long at that point. Consequently, I gave up writing until 2005 when I received a call from a guy called Dwain from Authorhouse.

Dwain explained that I had sent him a brief transcript (the first 3 chapters) some time ago and that he thought that it was worth merit. I explained that I had lost the file at which point he strongly recommended that I started to write again. Five years later, I completed my novel which is now on general E media (Kindle, Nook etc) called "Reaper of the Golden Sun" although I am thinking about changing the name to "The Dreamweaver" as no one seems to like a book with the name Reaper in the title.

Once I had completed the novel, I went back to poetry, which I really enjoy writing as it tends to be short bursts of creativity. This primarily suit's me as I have a very busy lifestyle. I enjoy writing poetry as most stuff comes from my deep embedded emotions. Not always particularly profitable but it tends to hit an accord with people.

Following on, I have just finished writing a children's book, entitled "The Magic Bubble", which is just presently having the cover being designed and then will be promoted. I am in the process of writing another novel loosely based around paganism and witchcraft, I am really enjoying this and get the feeling that it will be infinitely superior to anything else that I have written. Time will tell though!

My future goal is to see my Next novel, set in the 17/18th century through to its final publishing phase. I then want to write a further follow-on book, in order to finish the story. I have already planned the synopsis for the next book. I would then like to see it made as a film.

My next goal from that point would be to write a play for television. I have already started the plans for this, which is a drama/comedy. I would then like to continue writing books. My head is full of ideas, I love writing.

I consider myself to be quite sensitive and creative as a person, which I feel helps augment the quality of my writing. I honestly feel that the best is yet to come, that I can achieve great things in the literary world. I just need the chance, the money and the time.

60 THE BITTER SWEET BETRAYAL

Now linger this, the bitter taste of betrayal as learned friends
frown upon a friendship proved vile. Feel deep, the cold
sharp blade as woeful deeds cut savagely, piercing into my
warm glowing heart. Ponder no more, for the need of
memories past as emotions feed on fond deeds surpassed.
This I say, as tears I do weep, sullenly, slowly, down my red
embarrassed cheek.

Just a week ago, we laughed, we sighed, we played and cried,
was this a lie or some deluded game? I question my
judgement, my reasoning, why did I fall for this travesty -
would I do it all again?
I guess the answer, is predictably so, would I recognise the
signs, to be honest, I don't know! This I say, as tears I do
weep, sullenly, slowly, do.

Fool I be not, for my intentions were pure, if I fell from grace,
then the deception was clear. A short term gain, is a long term
loss, a misguided decision will turn sour and to cost. Yet it
pains me to recognise, the vulgarity of this act, no pride for
some from our historic pact.
This I say, as tears I do weep, sullenly, slowly, down my red
embarrassed cheek.

Laugh, may you laugh, gloat foolishly I cry, but hurt no more, my dented pride. My sullen face, with tears thus shed, down frown borne crevasses or so it's said. Thus wrinkles deep, from pain and hurt, a misspent deed from those undiscerned. This I say, as tears I do weep, sullenly, slowly, down my red embarrassed cheek.

Scathing, I curse, with vengeance this verse, in search for profanity, yet resentfully hurt. Although not alone am I in this world of victims, as I sufferer emotionally this deceit from within. Then a silence, a long unheard silence, with nothing to gain, as time's familiar task, sets to heal my pain. This I say, as tears I do weep, sullenly, slowly, down my red embarrassed cheek.

Mark Green ©

61 THE STREET

The work horse grafted, straining main and back. The monkeys jumped while the hyenas laughed. The pigs wallowed in their usual pit as the camels continued to un-hygienically spit. The dogs barked at all and sundry, the jelly fish quivered as it worked on Monday, the soldier ants marched for us all each day, while the farming sheep tended and gathered the hay.

The elephants continued to guard their tusks, the meerkats continued to feed on rusks, the ignorant vultures fed on fat cats as the innocent mice were chased by the rats. The tortoise again hid in his shell as the black panther, all sinister played in hell. The eagle eyed beagle walked the beat and the mountain rocked as the lion roared in the middle of the street.

This parody is clear and for all to see, the world around is no longer free, the animals rule with brainless tact as the rest of us live as a matter of fact. The news feeds us with knowledge and power as the clock ticks away hour by hour. As each second goes by, another chance lost, to alter the world and save the cost. The policemen continue to march the beat as the mountain rocked and the lion roared in the middle of the street.

62 YOU

The crispness of the morning as the frost bites the ground,
reminds me of a distant dream of a journey to another land,
where goodness doth prevail a warm and gentle kind, healing
all our ailments both of body and of mind.

I glance around the vista wide, upon this strange surreal view,
to recognise sweet berries red and hear the calling of the
shrew. Teardrops form from melting ice, signify a thaw, as
the sun smiles through a veil of cloud, a gift of life for all.

Footsteps in the virgin snow reveal another presence, through
trees and shrubs they wandered then disappeared into the
essence. Who is this guest I pondered, could it be friend or
perhaps a foe! As my mind guessed intuitively,
unsurprisingly, alas, I didn't know.

Then the wind kissed my moistened lips, as it breezed gently
by, hissing amongst the fallen leaves, ascending gracefully
into the sky. An eerie mist meandered through, a winding
mountain pass, writhing around my corporeal legs, offering a
slight scent of peat, marsh grass.

Heightened emotion, passive motion, feeling apprehension, as
lightness filled my weary head, my body taut with tension.
The crack of a twig, the roar of a bear, magnificent torso,

covered in hair. Standing proud, it glares at me then within a flash, just fled away.

My heart pounding, from this life changing moment, then silence and solace realign my emotions. "Where am I", I asked myself, feeling lonely and confused. Am I lost amongst this wilderness, or just dreaming in colourised hues?

Then I saw your face, in a familiar place, a friend and a lover true, and realised, to my surprise, that the whole of my life is you.

Mark Green ©

63 THE TREE OF HOPE

This ragged tree that hung so well, dismembered bodies in
their naked shells. That bore the scars of tightened rope,
which hung the men, devoid of hope. Mangled boughs,
matted leaves, tangled loosely within lichen sleeves.
Wind swept branches, reaching down, towards the blood
stained barren ground.
No life here in this wanton grave, whence cruel souls took but
never gave.

Thieves and highwaymen, soldiers of war, all fell victim to the
hangman's call. Innocent, guilty, husband or wife, had one
thing in common, a shortened life. Yet come it will, the kind
wind of change, that tempered the man, filled with guilt and
rage. No more to be sanctioned, such actions so vile, a new
sense of vision, trade scorn with smile.

New seasons come, new seasons go, the healing sun, white
deep cleansing snow. A birdsong from nest, young chicks
start to shrill, mother flies guardedly, in the early spring chill.
A sleepy river with deep banked mud pulls leafless twigs with
new grown buds. Swaying in time with ebbing grace, as the
ravens' brood, gaze deep into space.

A melodic call, pitch high, heard by all, beseeching harmony,
a plea to end war. Nature's force at its very best, no

thunderstorms here as harsh winds rest. Feel the heat heal our pain, the rain wash our stains, for this deed is done on this fine Sabbath day. Thus Innocent children, again they play, with their laughter and joy, stain colour into grey.

Thence the dawn of dreams as the blossom white, feeds scurrying bees whilst they buzz in flight. Sweet scented air, aromas rich, the rape, the wheat and the fine pollen stitch. Ethereal spirits dance gracefully around, this humble tree of deep hallowed ground. Whilst the children swing and gleefully sing under the old weeping willow's shroud.

Mark Green ©

64 SUNDOWN

Rhythmic drum beating to the distant shore as lapping waves clap for a sweet encore.

Blazing sun tempered by the beckoning night whilst willing eyes search patiently for the first starlight.

Dying embers of this magnificent feat fills the sky with deep coloured hues and passionate heat.

Bare toes sifting through fine golden sand, lamented lovers clasp palm into hand.

Soft mistral breeze, sway hair gently high as swerving seagulls glide effortlessly by.

A glass of white wine, crisp and cold, satisfies the taste buds of both young and old.

As we sit on the rocks, gazing out to sea, awaiting the finale of what will be, will be.

Smoked barbecues sizzle somewhere nearby, wafting sweet rich aromas as fine food fries.

Then the glowing orb, deep red glowing orb, sinks to the lost horizon, falling slowly down, this fading sun that this day did shine.

Anticipation, trepidation whilst we wait with sadness, yet filled with elation this incredible sight of nature's illusion.

Finally the prevailing darkness that defines the night as we glance one last time to the sad fading light that filled our hearts with joy for all, this fine summers day of wonder and awe.

Mark Green ©

Jaideep Khanduja

Jaideep writes under the pen name "Pebble In The Still Waters" on his two blogs http://pebbleinthestillwaters.in and http:// pebbleinthestillwaters.blogspot.com
He is an avid reader, book reviewer and keeps interviewing authors. He also writes short stories, haiku, memoirs and poetry.

65 HARE AND TORTOISE REVISTED IN 2015

This time, He decided,
I will not ditch my
challenger.
Even if he is sleeping,
I will wake him up
and will go fair
without thinking of stealing
the moment.

Earlier the rules of the game
were not clear,
the game was open
to be fought among
imbalanced expertise.
The challenger knew
I was weak on land
and I knew that he was weak
in water
but still I accepted his challenge
for land.

This time
I will again accept his challenge
on land

but will offer
a same challenge
for water
for the same distance.

And then let the
results
come
together
for land and water.

I promise
if he starts drowning
in water
I will take him
on my back
and will save his life
but will win the game
in revised preposition
of equality.

A Foe Turned Friend.

Jaideep Khanduja ©

66 BY THE TIME I REALIZED

Hello!
Do you know?
I have learnt to believe in you.
I have learnt though after a long time.

I also realized lately
that time is the key to everything.

By the time I realized
that I was thirsty for all these years
and water was not too far away,
eyes blurred with tears…

Jaideep Khanduja ©

67 HAIKU: PRAYER

Slurring thoughts in mind.
Slurping each day minute by minute.
Light blinded by dark.
Only 3 ways to enlighten dark.
Prayer, prayer and prayer.

Jaideep Khanduja ©

68 CAN YOU CLOSE YOUR EYES: TOUCH ME: AND TELL ME MY RELIGION?

Can you tell what is the religion of a word?
What caste a faith belongs to?
How to find out the difference in blood?
To whom an ocean belongs to?

Can you tell what is the religion of a mother?
Which caste of mother loves more to her child?
Which caste blood is more loyal?
Which caste brain works faster?

Can you tell how people belonging to different religions
have the same cycle of birth and death?
Can you tell why God didn't give different color
to blood of people belonging to different religions?

Why a doctor of one religion saves a patient
of different religion?
Why two soldiers of same religion standing
across borders kill each other?

Can you run a clock with different speed
for different religion?
Can you segregate oxygen in the air
religion wise?

Do you know the people who
play with religion, feelings and sentiments

belong to only one religion - cruelty, inhumanity, insanity.
Jaideep Khanduja ©

69 HAIKU: LAST KISS #DEATHISBEGINNING

Leaving a world of my own
to move into world of your thoughts.
A new beginning with
the last kiss of life
and first kiss of death.

Jaideep Khanduja ©

Ben Ditmars

Ben Ditmars is an author of gnomes, plays, poetry and more. He was first published in his college publications the Cornfield Review and KAPOW. Since then he has been featured in several online literary journals and heads the poetry committee at the Mid-Ohio Fine Art Society. Currently, he lives in Marion, Ohio and is working toward his Master's Degree. He loves historical documentaries and all things gnome.

70 BURN MY HEART

I take the black cup, and
I let it burn my heart.

I feel caffeine
rushing like addiction
in your pulse.

we live fast, when
we go slow.

moments
slip between
our fingers,

laced together
in the quiet hours

and they skip a beat,
sooner than we crash.

Ben Ditmars ©

71 DARKNESS IN HER SONG

there was darkness in
her song: a tender voice of
longing and despair
untouched by superstition
or the loss of innocence.

Ben Ditmars ©

72 FLUORESCENT IMPULSE

my impulse missed a
beat or two, submerged in life
the scent of perfume,
and fluorescent lights burned beige
from overuse: transcendence.

Ben Ditmars ©

73 RED LIGHTS

red light contradicts
blue sky and so much
depends on makeshift branches
set in stone, and her translucence
glazed with ice.

Ben Ditmars ©

74 CLOUDS ONE-THROUGH-NINE

doctors whisper through
the catheters and drain us in a
single use: infusion playing
on repeat, the television left
on church: a preacher speaks,
across syringes and we laugh
before the anesthesia kills
clouds one-through-nine.

Ben Ditmars ©

Aric Cushing

Aric Cushing is the writer of *The Yellow Wallpaper* feature film, and has starred in a variety of film, television shows, and videos since the 1990's. He studied at the American Conservatory for the Arts, and the London Court Theater in England. While researching the companion novel for *The Yellow Wallpaper* film, he discovered two previously lost stories by literary reformer Charlotte Perkins Gilman, currently in the volume *Charlotte Perkins Gilman: The Complete Gothic Collection*. As an actor, his film *Runs in the Blood* is set to be released in 2015, along with the horror zombie flick, *Breakdown Lane*, and his middle grade novel, *Vampire Boy*. His favorite author is Honore Balzac, and his favorite dog, without doubt, is the Pugenstein.

75 GUTTER TALK

No more lies among the roses, please —
My hands grip tight the thorns,
And bleed.

Out of some darkness,
And a little rain,
Come the pitter patter of the rats to feed.

I've already given you all my pains,
Why wait any longer?
Go ahead and stab me to death.
At least I'll have my parting breath —

You already have, I know, you know,
Blood streams in the drains,
And wanes.

What the hell,
I'm dead in the gutter. That sucks.
My love was less than all that combined,
Devoured among the roses, where the weeds entwine.

Aric Cushing ©

76 MIDNIGHT SCREAMS

Awakened at night by cries, screams.
I believe at first it is a dream.
But it is not. It is a scream.

"Stop it. I mean it! Stop!"
And I twist and turn,
Blankets not blanketing the sound from my ears.

Another scream, and scuffling, fills the years.
It is my roommates past midnight,
Biting harsh bitter, stinging tears.

I am now fully awake, blinking to the sky.
My message machine winking, pounding.
A strange, dull light.

Who could have called me before the screams?
"Stop crying! I mean it! Stop!"
Life is a never-ending flow of burnt-out dreams.

My roommate's lover is in the kitchen by the sink.
His face is battered, bloody, and fat.
I give him water to sip from, like a dying cat.

Could he have finally called me in my sleep?
When I was hiding from life's worries,
Shuttered and closed, from dreams.

There is crying again from the room next to mine.
They are lost – "Why can't you just take care of me?"
I pray for a voice to scream at me. "Fine!"

Life is the worn-out days of time,
Flowing after midnight, wicked puzzles—Ha! Stupid rhymes.
Are you—?

I stare at the message machine hoping it is—
Listen—
Life is a never-ending flow of burnt-out dreams,
Life is a mixture of our midnight screams.

Aric Cushing ©

77 THE SECOND TIME WE MET

The second time we met
You did not bring your eyes to mine
You looked so different . . .
God, how different I cannot say!

The sparkle and flicker of passion gone,
The longing and excitement you emanated from before
All gone, far gone, you looked so different and alone.

The second time we met
I wanted to bring you close to me
To make you put down your rent and bills, life's papers
To hug you close. To set you free.

"It's 8:15. I thought you weren't coming."
I did not know what to say
The terrible door shut close behind me.

I followed you up the stairs, long and thick
Carpeted with your sorrow
Had it come and gone so quick?

But I listened, I did, not fearing you —
Speak of your life and your kids.
Among the dim light of that crappy café
My heart still beating, trying not to wither away.

I looked to myself, doubled, and checked
I rushed into things, you said
And held in my pain
Please don't tell me these things again.

You see, that night I wanted to tell you
Before you answered the door
Of visions lost and gained
Languishing on the shore.

"Stop now," I wanted to say, relinquish, as before
Do not hide in the black remains
Of life's terrible door.

That night I wanted to drive you —
Far and away to some distant land,
Never to be burdened, never to be weighed
From Life's terrible demands.

To take you in my arms and love you
Cajole, hug, cuddle you tight
To never let you go, to the dawn's early light.

You are a lion, a bull, so strong, with no fear
"Do not worry," I wanted to say,
"I am here."

But I said nothing instead, sat in silence and tears
Wondering what I could say, what I could do
To help you from your fears.

There was nothing
This was the second time we met
Your face was clouded from life's vicious net.

It was fear. Fear, let me tell you, harsh and dark.
The opening of sea chambers —
Black blood of mistaken hearts.

Aric Cushing ©

78 THE MUSIC AT THE END

Can I hold you now, I said.
We stood in a dark club where we could finally live.
Me falling through some weird sieve.

'Whatever' you say,
I pulled my hand away.
I guess there's nothing more to say.

Aric Cushing ©

79 THE GIAOUR'S LAMENT

From a blackened tomb he comes again,
Eyes red and grey from a history spent.
Aquiline nose with darkened locks,
Face cold and grim from life's hard knocks—

The world has changed, "didn't you know", again as before,
Lost in a coma of texting and more.
The gowns are packed up in the vault,
At Vogue.

The age old romance of kissing is dead,
Scratching at the window for death to wed.
Your kin has been cheapened.
Your legend weakened.
The modern are all but lost in their heads.

Back to the tomb you'd better go,
Terror is no longer the best-in-show.
Vampires are pretty and plucky and fun,
Your legend is lost, and the machines have won.

Aric Cushing ©

Jill M. Roberts

As a native New Yorker, Jill has had great opportunities and access to fine arts. She's traveled throughout Europe and spent her twenties residing half in London and New York. As a poet, Jill's work is quite personal and thus is filled with raw emotion. After battling cancer, she finally found a love unlike any other. Tragedy struck once more when on holiday in England, Jill lost her love to an unknown heart condition. She returned to New York alone and filled with despair. As only she can, Jill put pen to paper and turned the experience into prose. A few pieces will be published here and the rest of the collection will be in her book, Losing Innocence. You can see her published books on her website, www.JillMRoberts.com. Jill still resides on the Upper East Side of Manhattan with her children Liam and Emma.

80 ONE LIFE

I sit and await the anniversary of the terror;
The abhorrent morning that I woke to another world.
A world where you cease to exist in mine.
That morning will reside with me always,
Wherever I am or Whatever I do.

Awaking to the awful sound
Your struggling breath.
Running to your side of our bed,
Pulling you close,
Only to lose you in my arms.
Your breath left your body,
One last time.
Sleeping eyes that woke lifeless.
Hope,
Leaving my soul,
With dread and panic taking its place.
You see, it was hopeless,
I knew you were gone.
The emergency response did not have to rush.
They did their job regardless,
But to no avail.

I stood over you,
Watching and helping the revival process.
My world shattered,
I missed you already.

That moment,
When you were freed of the physical,
I became chained,
To a life of misery.
Life here without you,
A karmic debt hugely paid.

I am left now to dwell amongst the anonymous.
My head down, my heart heavy.
I wonder along the streets we walked;
Remembering everything said and shared.
You, the balance in my life,
Making it all worthwhile.
The one man who has loved me,
Unconditionally and unselfishly.
You were security,
You made everything alright.
An anesthetic, a conqueror, my protector.

You,
Died,
On a Saturday morning,
Nearing two years ago.
I,
Died,
There with you.
Both of us lost to this world,
But living in parallel universes.
Yours, a new journey,
Stepping on to the shore of Heaven,
Mine, still here,
Existing in shadows
Of the darkness of Hell.

Jill M. Roberts ©

81 A MOMENT OF HAPPINESS

It started out as an ordinary day,
Any ordinary day in one's life.
We had probably been out the night before,
This memory escapes me now.
We woke to coffee and cigarettes
As we usually did.

You were on the Gucci site
Showing me the style of suit you had wanted.
We decided to hit Gucci on 5th Avenue.
Parenthetically, if you remember,
I wore sweats and a T-shirt, and you,
You wore your father's old suit which kept it's wear.
Here we were, walking toward Gucci,
Debating on whether I should visit Iceland on holiday.

Outside the store,
We were one of the anonymous,
But inside, we stepped into another world,
One of the rich, on 5th Avenue in New York City
Where price tags do not exist.
I remember the elevator ride and our conversation.
Stepping out to be greeted by a salesperson,
Whom I ordered around and kept on his toes due to his thirst
for a sale.

A vision of you,

Standing there in the suit chalked up by the tailor.
I handed you a wine glass filled with Pelligrino,
To wash down the Xanax forced into your mouth.
When all was done, we were outside again,
Amongst the anonymous.

Later that night, we sat at the Whiskey Bar celebrating our day.
I remember hearing glimpses of U2's "Beautiful Day"
In the background and thinking how appropriate.
I thought this was the beginning of happiness,
And there would always be more.
It was happiness, the moment.
All our feelings, yours and mine, all mixed up.
The madness of it all.
You see I wanted to give you it all, the world if possible.
To make you happy, in every viable platform.
I know now you didn't feel the same.
Left with everything unsaid and undone between us.

Having that one day with you was my moment of happiness.
You have given all you had to offer for me.
For us.
I am here and you are there,
A huge distance between us.
Know, even though we have not spoken,
I am here,
For the conversation, the friendship, the silence.
Remember always what I said to you before I fled to England,
The night we walked the promenade;
Love doesn't end just because we don't see one another.
No matter how you look at it,
It's only Love after all.

Jill M. Roberts ©

82 THE POWER OF THOUGHT

You view me as malicious,
Intending on wounding ones in my path.
You're wrong, it's just circumstance.
Circumstance has made me pay the price.
Now it's time I hop off the wheel of suffering.
Offer up my faux pas, mistakes, oversights
Whatever you may call it.

It is time for peace.
Peace within.
For time does not exist.
And life is eternal.
We make our own heaven and hells
Here on Earth.
We make that choice.
I and we must become righteous and change.
The power of thought is resilient.
It's the ego, who wants to hold on with all its force
To keep us in fear.
It is time for peace within.

So you are mistaken with your "knowingness" of me
And your philosophies are the same.
Time for change.
Yes; however not the type of change you infer.
I do not need to be knocked down by you,
You who think that all the answers are there –

Move, cut people out, etc…
The answer is within my essence.
My problems are miniscule in comparison
To the real problem.
The separation from God and my brothers.

If I change my thoughts to one with Him,
All the right people and things will come into my life.
I won't keep making same mistakes with the same people.
For all I can do is try and be patient.
Put my talent to use,
And not "die with my music still in me".
I owe it to God, myself and my audience
To make an impression.
Do what I was put here to do.

Pain is easier to write than happiness.
We all can validate pain effortlessly.
But it is the Joy and Happiness that should be validated.
Most of us are stuck, here, in a place where the darkness
Seems like it will last forever.
That is our choice, our misperception.
We can change by seeing the good and innocence in people,
Even when it's hard.
Love cannot be taught, it is something we own.
Send love or send fear.
God has granted free will.
From now on I choose Heaven and peace.
From now on I choose to send Love.

Jill M. Roberts ©

83 CASTLE IN THE SKY

In the summer of my days,
I sit alone on a chaise in the bedroom.
Clothes draped,
Books as cue,
And my chest heavy from my burdens.
How will this all end?
The inevitable question.
Deemed to be alone forever?
I dare not to consider this.
Suppose, is to assume I've lost heart.
For not is my will to strive for passion.
He's somewhere I have not looked.
I agreed to be found
But stuck in a labyrinth to test my fate.
At the door he awaits to seize me
And share me with no other.
I am aware of the existence of love.
The love that is already all around me;
Yet it does not come easy.
The sun strikes the afternoon position.
I lie upon my chaise and fall into slumber
Like a potion has been ingested.
My lover calls to me,
In my castle in the sky.
I try to run to him,
The fog is too thick
I cannot be seen.

I move to the sweet sound of his voice.
There is a gate in the mists.
I cannot gain access.
I try and fall.
Though I persist.
I yearn to be with him.
I must find him
He ought to reveal his identity.
I see a vague figure,
Far beyond the gate.
I cry out to him
Pleading to let me in.
My heart pounds so hard
It leaves ringing in my ears.
My veins pulsate with adrenaline
My stomach is hatching butterflies.
He starts toward me
"Yes!" I think,
Soon he'll be revealed to me.
As he ascends from the entrance hall,
I begin to be pulled back.
Quickly blinded and yanked away.
"No!" I scream,
But he doesn't seem to hear me.
I try to grab onto the gate,
My hands slipping,
I cannot take hold.
He is becoming farther and further away.
And then my eyes open.
It is then,
I realize it was just a dream.
He is lost to me forever.
Out of breath I seize the glass.
Gasping, I take a sip

Then smash it against the fireplace.
With my head in my hands I look up;
Panting and yearning
To be free.

Jill M. Roberts ©

84 LOSING INNOCENCE

Why do we risk it all for love?
No matter how exquisite,
Passionate, wonderful it is,
We lose;
Always.
Whether we part for differences or in death,
We lose;
Always.
No matter how much we try to hold on,
Change ourselves or our other,
Govern and protect the relationship,
We lose;
Always.
Thus, why do we do it?
We do it for the moments that will reside with us,
Always.

For the craze and lust.
The fury,
The fervor,
The obsession, infatuation, excitement.
For the zeal, enthusiasm, passion.
We do it for us;
To penetrate over into,
Our partner.
Me and You,
We wanted it all.

None of the pain,
Just the good stuff.
Well, we had it.
The good, the lovely.
What a surprise!
But then,
As Always,
We lost.

We lost ourselves,
Our way.
The rhythm and balance
We perfected.
How did we not see it coming?
Stumbling on to a new realm.
One in which we operate alone.
The composition wrecked.
We smashed into that brick wall.
Afraid to leave,
Co-dependent.
I knew you wanted out.
Maybe a break?
You opposed it.
We could not come back from it.
I could feel the coming loss.
But not in the way I expected.

A trip!
To get us back.
The excitement could mend us.
It did for 72 hours.
Then the ultimate force of depature
Came upon.
In a small elegant English hotel,
You died in my arms

On a Saturday morning in London.
Thirty five hundred miles away from home.

The initial shock blasted my mind and body.
The detonation of torment pierced my soul.
Unadulterated suffering terrorized.
I lost my equilibrium and steadiness.
Embarking in an unknown world,
Where the dwellers seethe with agony.
A spot was saved for me there,
Where fumes suffocate.
A Hell on Earth
Where Innocence is Lost.

Jill M. Roberts ©

Aaron L. Speer

Aaron L Speer was born and raised in Sydney and has been writing since his early childhood, a drawback of only being interested in English at school. His marks reflected this, causing his teachers to pray he would become a writer so as not to be completely destitute. His novel Night Walker, an Australian vampire novel, was published in September 2014. He currently lives with his fiancé in Blakehurst, Sydney, working on his sequel Day Dreamer.

85 ASHLEE

You repaired my heart
And changed my life.
You'll delight me again
When you become my wife.

Though I wait for our greatest feat,
The day that our family becomes complete,

Every day I close my eyes and whisper my heartfelt vow.
The same promise I make now.
I will always love you.

Aaron L. Speer ©

Isabella J. Mansfield

Isabella J. Mansfield is a freelance writer and poet. She writes mostly to clear her head, using words to work through some of life's little, and sometimes not-so-little frustrations. Her debut poetry collection, "At Arm's Length", was published December 2014, and she is currently working on her second book. She currently lives in Phoenix, AZ with her husband and son.

86 TENTH

When I kissed you
I closed my eyes.
Not because it felt
Nice, though it did,
But because I was
Afraid to open them
And see how much
You had changed.

Isabella J. Mansfield ©

87 TINY POCKET TEE

We all wore them then,
Silly little shirts
That hugged our curves
Sometimes a little too tightly.

I had one with a tiny little pocket
And I could feel your eyes
Burning a hole into it as
You looked and looked.

When you finally spoke,
You asked what good it was,
Such a tiny little thing, it barely fit
The nickel you dared to slip inside it.

Isabella J. Mansfield ©

88 YOUR NEW SHOES

The way you held my hand
Was not tender or even kind.
But full of malice
And you would not
Let me go.

I poured my heart out
To you, but it spilled
And sloshed
And splashed
And made a mess of things.

You were upset;
It had soiled your new shoes,
Shiny and black.
The ones you bought
Just to walk all over me.

Isabella J. Mansfield ©

89 HANDS

Your hands felt
Different
Than I was used to.
Smoother,
Without fingerprints.
I expected they
Would not leave
A mark on me.
But they did.

Isabella J. Mansfield ©

90 THE SMELL OF GRAPEFRUIT

I had this soap once.
It wasn't particularly special
but it smelled like citrus,
grapefruit especially,
and I liked the way it
made me feel so
exhilarated.

At the time, I would
experience that same
exhilaration whenever
you said my name.

Olfactory memory is
such a funny thing.
Even now, the smell of
grapefruit makes me
catch my breath in
anticipation.

Isabella J. Mansfield ©

THE END

ABOUT THE PUBLISHER

Star Investment Strategies LLC. has branched out into publishing authors in various genres from around the globe. Mirrored Voices : Emerging Poets Anthology is the first ever piece of literature produced with multiple authors to date. It is the stepping stone for a fruitful future. Star Investment Strategies stands proud to be investing in the stars.

Website: Paul-Morabito.com

Made in the USA
Middletown, DE
26 January 2015